When Winter Come

Kentucky Voices

Buffalo Dance: The Journey of York
Frank X Walker

The Cave
Robert Penn Warren

Famous People I Have Known
Ed McClanahan

Miss America Kissed Caleb
Billy C. Clark

Sue Mundy: A Novel of the Civil War
Richard Taylor

The Total Light Process: New and Selected Poems
James Baker Hall

When Winter Come: The Ascension of York
Frank X Walker

With a Hammer for My Heart: A Novel
George Ella Lyon

When Winter Come

The Ascension
of York

Frank X Walker

THE UNIVERSITY PRESS OF KENTUCKY

Publication of this volume was made possible in part by a grant from the National Endowment for the Humanities.

The following poems first appeared (some in slightly different form) in *We Proceeded On*, the journal of the Lewis and Clark Trail Heritage Foundation, in January 2007: "In the Name a the Father," "The River Speaks," "Watkuweis Speaks," "Art of Seduction," "Lovers' Moon," "Primer II," "Praying Feets," "Murmuration," "Field Up," "Unwelcome Guest," "Real Costs," "Umatilla Prophecy," and "Eye of the Beholder."

Published 2008 by The University Press of Kentucky
Scholarly publisher for the Commonwealth,
serving Bellarmine University, Berea College, Centre College of Kentucky, Eastern Kentucky University, The Filson Historical Society, Georgetown College, Kentucky Historical Society, Kentucky State University, Morehead State University, Murray State University, Northern Kentucky University, Transylvania University, University of Kentucky, University of Louisville, and Western Kentucky University.
All rights reserved.

Editorial and Sales Offices: The University Press of Kentucky
663 South Limestone Street, Lexington, Kentucky 40508-4008
www.kentuckypress.com

12 11 10 09 08   5 4 3 2 1

Library of Congress Cataloging-in-Publication Data

Walker, Frank X, 1961–
  When winter come : the ascension of York / Frank X Walker.
    p. cm. — (Kentucky voices)
  Includes bibliographical references.
  ISBN 978-0-8131-2483-4 (acid-free paper)
  ISBN 978-0-8131-9184-3 (pbk. : acid-free paper)
  1. York, ca. 1775–ca. 1815—Poetry. 2. Lewis and Clark Expedition (1804–1806)—Poetry. 3. West (U.S.)—Discovery and exploration—Poetry. 4. African American men—Poetry. 5. Explorers—Poetry.
  6. Slaves—Poetry. I. Title.
  PS3623.A359W47 2008
  813'.6—dc22   2007037305

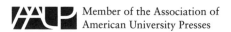 Member of the Association of
American University Presses

For Jade Imani Chiles
and all our Native Sons (and Daughters)
. . . may they recognize home when they find it.

It will be useful to acquire what knowledge you can of
the state of morality, religion & information among them,
as it may better enable those who endeavor to civilize and
instruct them . . .

—*Thomas Jefferson's instructions*
to Meriwether Lewis, June 1803,
from The Journals of Lewis and Clark

The federal attack on Indian self determination during
the 19th Century included the forcible displacement of tribes,
the creation of a reservation system, and the
more subtle devaluation of Indian cultures and histories.

—*from* Oxford History
of the American West

Contents

Part II

Introduction

In 1803, President Thomas Jefferson instructed Lewis and Clark to explore the Missouri River to its source, establish the most direct land route to the Pacific, and make scientific and geographical observations. In the interests of trade and peace, they also were to learn what they could of the Indian tribes they encountered and impress them with the strength and authority of the United States.

After meeting in Louisville, enlisting the first permanent members of the party—nine young men from Kentucky—and heading down the Ohio, up the Mississippi, and to the Wood River, Lewis and Clark spent the winter training the recruits and preparing for their ascent up the Missouri. On May 14, 1804, the Corps of Discovery officially launched the exploration phase of the great trek west and reached the ocean almost a year and a half later in November 1805.

Along the way they would encounter various tribes of Native Americans, many of whom contributed to the success of the journey. While the twenty-eight-month long, eight thousand mile journey to the ocean and back set the stage for expansion and migration that would soon follow, it was the beginning of irrevocable and devastating changes for Native people.

By 1830—just twenty-four years after the Lewis and

Clark expedition—the newly passed Indian Removal Act had forcibly relocated many eastern tribes across the Mississippi River into Indian Territory and what is now present-day Oklahoma. Between 1778 and 1868, the United States government executed nearly 800 treaties with American Indian nations. Of these, fewer than 370 were ratified by the Congress, leaving many tribes landless and without formal recognition or acknowledgement. Since 1778, over 2.2 billion acres of Indian lands have been ceded to the United States. Today, 2.5 percent of original lands, or 56 million acres, remain in tribal jurisdiction. The last treaty was signed in 1868, forcing Chief Joseph and his Nez Perce followers to move from the Wallowa Valley in Oregon.

Inspired by visits to the Nez Perce reservation, communication with York's Nez Perce descendents, and transcribed Nez Perce oral history, this book is about deconstructing accepted notions of history, love, marriage, and freedom while simultaneously reaffirming the power of literacy and the role of mythology and storytelling in exploration of the truth. It seeks to validate the voices of enslaved African Americans and Native peoples during a time in American history when their points of view were considered invalid. In this way, it seeks to fill a gap in the collective works about the Lewis and Clark expedition and its other important but often overlooked figures.

Glossary

Gye Nyame
Akan symbol for the omnipotence and omnipresence of God

Ile-Ife
spiritual capital of Yorubaland, center of creation

'Legba (Elegba)
Orisa of mischief, the trickster

Oludumare
Yoruba reference for Almighty God

Orisa (Orisha)
divine being

Tse-mook-tse-mook To-to-kean
Nez Perce for black Indian

Watkuweis
Nez Perce for "she who returned from a far-away country"

Yemaya
Orisa of the sea and maternal love

Opening

Role Call

Role Call

To hear hero makers tell it
wasn't nobody
on the great expedition but captains.
An them always mentions Seaman
Capt. Lewis's dog
before them remembers me.

Beneath the captains was three sergeants
though something evil got in the bowels
a Sgt. Floyd an took his life, barely a year
after joining up. I was sorry to see him pass.

Among almost two dozen privates
was a sharp young boy no more than eighteen
a couple a blacksmiths
an several Virginy an Kentucke mens
that knowed they way 'round furs an skins.

We had us a couple a Frenchmans
born an raised as Indians.
Most a them could shoot straight an some
was pretty good hunters, though none
could best me.

An though alla the books praise the captains
the most valuable members a the party
was even lower than privates, but be

the ones that saved all our lives
more than a time or two.

The real heroes be old cowardly Charbono's young squaw
an Drewyer, another man full a both French
an Indian blood.

They was the best at talking with they hands
bargaining with the Indians along the way
an quieting the killer we sometime seen in they eyes.

Sacagawea was best at finding roots to eat when we
was near starving an one a the ones to steer us right
when we was lost.

An then, there was me, just along to cook an carry,
to hear them tell it, but there be two sides to ev'ry story
an then there be the truth.

This story be born a my own spit an memory
it be the only thing I own outright
an I gives it to you freely.

Homecoming

> You will be at ease only in your own home.
> —*African proverb*

After I visits villages a families
in charge a themselves
meets barefoot warriors an chiefs
listens to wisdom a storytellers
an medicine men, an see people
married to the earth
fishing the rivers an living off the land

dancing an singing in circles
wearing animal masks
caressing voices
out a skin-headed drums an rattles

honoring them ancestors
an them toothless at the beginning
an at the end a life

I wonder if all the stories Ol' York told
on the porch, was really 'bout
ol' Africa
or just a conjurer's way a planting seeds
so his son recognize home
when he see it.

The Melting

Ol' York say Mandingo, Ibo, Dogon
Akan, Yoruba, an more be chained together
in the bottom a boats
an brought to this land

He say one a the tricks used
to make a man a slave
an kill his language
be to take away the name
he call hisself

When I listens to the Sioux, the Hidatsa
Arikara, Mandan, Shoshone, Salish,
Chinook, an even the Nez Perce
all be called savage

Indian, red man, or chil'ren
by the captains
I wonders how long it take before
they answers to niggah too.

The Great Inquisition

Some answers come so easy
the questions be barely worth asking.

Some things root in the back
ova man's head,
wrestle him in the dark
an follow him 'round
for the rest a his life:

Why I never run to freedom?

How my heart make room
for two women?

When I come to know God?

An what did I pretends not to know
'bout the men an the facts
a the great expedition?

I've studied on these same questions
for many a year, struggled with some
a the answers, an eventually come to terms
with all they truths
no matter who ear them sting.

Part I

In the Name

In the Name a the Father

Them call the old guide that led us
through the mountains, *Toby,*
Sacagawea, *Janey,*
her lil' Jean Baptiste, *Pomp,*
an me *boy,* an worse if it cross they minds.

Them call the beautiful Nimiipuu
Nez Perce though we never seen a pierced nose
in the mountains or plains.

Them give a name to ev'ry stream an place
we come 'cross
even named a group a small islands after me
without ever thinking to ask the people
who lived there if they already had names.

What is it, I wonder
gets in a white man's head so
that when him look in the mirror
him always see God

but when him look at people
with hair like lambs wool
or feet a burnt brass
him see only devils or chil'ren.

River Like a Snake

How the River Like a Snake

> Whoever sees the snake and does not flee, plays with
> death.
>
> —*Yoruba Proverb*

She turn right then left then right again
some time circling 'round to almost where we begin.
She make us dodge sharp trees an rocks

underwater logs an moving sand bottoms.
We pushes an pulls the keelboats an big canoes
the whole day long just to travel a distance

a man can cover on foot in a few minutes.
She put me in mind ova long mean snake
that swallow a pack a field mouses.

An while we trys to find our way out her stomach
she swallow sticks an rocks an enough cold water
to keep us in her belly long enough for us to pass.

My captain an the men laughs at my fear
a the river an my singing her apologies
an prayers at night an while we works

but I know she alive an I know she do all
she can to break our spirits an make the party
change they minds an give up the expedition.

But she don't know that a company
a rugged men who take well to orders
is as fearless an hard-headed as she is long an deep.

The River Speaks

My soul has grown deep like the rivers.
—*Langston Hughes*

call me the ohio, the mississippi, or the missoura
    call me wood, teton, yellowstone, milk, judith, marias,
    jefferson, madison, beaverhead, bitterroot, snake,
    clearwater, or pallouse
        call me the wide-toothed mouth of the columbia river
        call me after my many creeks
        my great falls
        my hot springs

            i am the snow atop mt. adams
            i am the salty hope in the air
                at cape disappointment
            i am she who is the deep and the shallows
            a thundering waterfall and a quiet storm
        i am always present in the air, on every tongue
    in every drop of milk and blood and tear
    you will find me in every thorn and flower   seed and fruit
    there is no life without me

    i am libation and baptismal pool
        i am your sprinkle of holy water
        i am older than man and light
            i am of god not god
                but like god, i am also inside of every man
                for all are born in me and form there until

they are flushed naked into the world
and i remain there in them like god
until they depart and return to dust

captain clark saw me
as a great wet road that could be conquered
with the rowing and paddling of men
under his command
so i showed him
my many rapids and waterfalls
made his men carry their own boats
and supplies around me for miles at a time
these were the good years
white men had not yet studied the beaver
and learned how to redirect my paths
manage my flow   harness it for their own use
attempt to enslave me too

captain lewis was different.
to him i was a piece of art
he marveled at the natural
falling of my waterlocks and felt humbled
by the beautifully carved rock masterpieces
that adorn my canyons and walls

while i have been at most an open way
for the white man
to the red man
i have been viewed as a helpmate
considered a wife
carrying their salmon and trout
providing for their
transportation and nourishment
surrounding them
moving through them
in the heat of the sweat lodge

answering their prayers
  when they dance

    but the black one was the only one
    taught to both fear and respect me
    and though i was the road
    that carried the ships of death
    to and from africa's shores
    i became the waiting outstretched arms
    for those who refused
    to be enslaved
    for those who trusted me
    to rock their babies off to sleep

my ocean floors   are covered   with   his people's   resistance
  i carry their spirit   in every   splash i make

  their humming
   their lost voices
    their last words
      have become a part
    of my sweetest songs

    when he is whole
  again
  when york knows
    what he is worth, i will well up inside
      of him   and he   will hear
        them sing.

Watkuweis Speaks

We knew they were coming.
Our medicine men have been telling
of their arrival since before I was born.

When our warriors saw their small herd
their first thoughts were to kill them all
and with it the destruction they carried.

This I also believed they should do
until I saw the black one
standing off to the side

a small mountain
pretending to be a man
a man pretending to be on a leash.

To the unlearned eye he looked to be all alone
but when I stared at him with my spirit eye
I could see a great long woman standing behind him

with her arms crossed
and a herd of strange-looking buffalo
large black cats, striped horses

and other wild beasts like I'd never even seen
in my dreams
stretching to where the sun rises.

17

I did not know what destruction his death
would earn us, so I counseled against it
and talked of the white men who were kind to me

when I was young and lost
which caused the warriors to put away their weapons
and welcome them with open arms.

Without Bibles

> We were taught generosity to the poor and reverence
> for the Great Mystery. Religion was the basis for all
> Indian training.
>
> —*Ohiyesa, Santee Sioux*

Massa call them heathens
when them clean they naked flesh
with ice cold mountain water
before crawling backward
into a dark hot hole in the earth
like they crawling back in the woman
who first give them life

sit there an suffer in thick steamy darkness
with other naked men
just to sweat an pray
sweat an sing
sweat an sweat an sweat

all the while asking blessings for they family, yours
they enemy, the land, the water, plants
an all the animals them share the earth with.

Sitting in a river a sweat
be no more than bathing to the captains
but a blind man can see God
in everything the red man do.

Whupped

Whupped

When the Mandan try to kill his wife
for lying with Sgt. Ordway, it cause
the captains to place married squaws
off-limits to the men's private commerce.

One a them laugh an brag 'bout having his way
with a daughter ova chief
for no more than a empty tobacco box.

When we learn the Indians believe
our power can change hands an be gifted
by passing 'tween a woman's thighs

we all takes advantage at every occasion
an in most every village
all along the great trip out an back

With Capt. Clark's permission, I don't hesitate
to enjoy myself an even have my nose opened
by a Nez Perce woman as beautiful
an rugged as the land we traveling through.

Like a Virgin

Grown folk don't walk 'round on the plantation
holding hands, go for canoe rides or take long walks
with each other.

My Nez Perce gal was the first woman I chose
on my own an that I didn't have to share with another.

I find myself staring into her eyes an smiling, learning
my big buffalo self to move like a turtle in her arms.

Men in the party think it strange that I not brag
'bout how many ways or how long we ride each other.

This way a being with a woman be so new an tender
I close my eyes an feel like a fresh born calf stumbling
on weak wet legs, discovering that it not the ground
that be moving.

Like Raven

Like Raven from Head to Toe

York's Nez Perce wife

His hair and strength was not unlike
that of the wooly-headed buffalo.

Some of my people thought
he had been burned by a great fire

Others thought he had painted
himself in charcoal, as was the custom

for warriors returning from the warpath
making him the bravest among his party.

Two hard wet fingers did not remove
the black from his forehead or arms

nor did the sweat from our naked turtle dance
make his salty skin any less like the night.

Art of Seduction

York's Nez Perce wife

I know a hungry man's eye can undress a woman
from across a smoldering fire, because York did it.

When I grew warm to his advances,
I gave him permission and invited him over

without ever opening my mouth. I looked away,
then back, then away, then back, so slow

when my eyes returned to meet his,
it made his nostrils flare and my heart beat

like two drums in my chest.
He didn't have a courting flute, so the first music we made

between us was a way of looking into each other's eyes
and exchanging naked promises so full of heat

passers-by would swear we were already man and wife.
His big hands were rough from a life full of hard work

but when they were filled with me
each one became a party of men deep in the wilderness

intent on exploring every mound
and knowing all of the hollowed-out and sacred places.

Quiet Storm

Quiet Storm
York's Nez Perce wife

> . . . may the moon softly restore you by night, may
> the rain wash away your worries . . .
> —*Apache blessing*

While out searching for camas and other roots
to celebrate our choosing each other

I made pictures with my fingers and lips
trying to make the raven's son understand

the number and beauty of the butterfly.

A rainstorm came out of the hills and forced us
to crawl under a giant pine's outstretched wings.

The soft bed of needles under us and the music
in the steady downpour left us so warm and wet

we barely noticed when the rain stopped
and moved on across the valley.

Before our lips and tongues finally parted
we floated like two eagles circling midair

trying to pass off a just-caught salmon
a mile above the Clearwater.

Lovers' Moon

York's Nez Perce wife

After the redheaded one's bed is made
and his stomach full of meat, he gives

my Tse-mook-tse-mook To-to-kean the slice of
daylight left to do as he pleases.

Pretending not to rush back to me
he passes by and nods.

After I track him down in the dark, jump on
his back and wrestle him to the ground

we wander off laughing toward the horses
then follow the riverbank upstream, holding hands

and looking for a private place to celebrate
the way the moon dances on the face of the water.

We find a rock to hold all our clothes
and play in the shallows like children

but after our bodies kiss, we stop to weigh
the gift of time alone and grow up real fast.

Midnight Ride

York's Nez Perce wife

After the fires die down, a moon full of shine
allows us to wander off into the night's arms.

Urged on by the river
and the night's music, our two quickly become one.

Straddled aboard him
a buffalo robe around my shoulders and nothing else

I close my eyes and ride
low and close, the way a hunter tracks buffalo

in the deep winter snow.
Our gentle trot becomes a gallop and after a good sweat

our gallop becomes
a quiet stand. Then we bow our heads an wait

for our breaths to catch up.
After a quick dip in the cold river, I mount back up

for warmth and we ride slow
and long until my legs quiver and York finds the strength

to harness himself.
When he carries me back home to our mat

folded up in his arms like a child
we lie down in the lap of the night

both empty and full   and sleep.

Circle a Gifts

Circle a Gifts

> Goodrich has recovered from "the Louis Veneri"
> [syphilis] . . . I cured him as I did Gibson last winter
> by the uce of mercury.
> —*Meriwether Lewis, January 27, 1806*

The men in the party don't know
that the white men who come first left a gift
Capt. Lewis believe he can cure

with something he call mercury
'til the men start to lose they sight.
Them be surprised when a ax we trade

come back to meet us many miles and moons
up the M'soura, but even bigger surprises return

after we travels all the way to the ochian
an trade lil' pieces a ribbon an trinkets
for a good time 'tween young Chinook thighs

Surprises that return to the givers
like a rabid bear easing out ova winter cave.

Forsaking All Others

York's Nez Perce wife

Babies have mothers to feed them
and keep them warm

Old men have children
to comfort their slow gray years

What kind of man needs another man
to carry him food, make his bed

and pack his things
and him not lame or blind?

What kind of man
makes one with such big medicine

pretend to be a child
and less?

How will he treat our warriors when
he does not need our food to stay alive?

I want to spit on the ground
when he comes near.

I can not respect the redheaded one
and honor my black man too.

Meteorology

I finds myself returning
to the sweat lodge at night
asking these beautiful an kind people's
Great Spirit
to heap nothing but blessings
upon his red chil'ren
almost as much as I wish for even more snow
to keep us here long enough
to see my woman's belly swell
with the only gift
I can leave her an them.

A nappy lil' new York
who will only know
one Massa.

The one that give an protect life
an not the one
that make men slaves.

Capt. Lewis pace back an forth
Massa Clark cuss the whole day
at the deep mountain snow that stand
'tween us an the great plains.

Them both worry that us all grow too fat
an lazy to finish the journey home.

False Impressions

False Impressions
York's Nez Perce wife

for Craig Howe

When winter comes, my people circle up and agree
on the most important thing that happened in the year,
an awful flood, an important battle, or the passing

of a great warrior, and boil it down to a picture
scratch it out on rawhide, and charge the storyteller
with remembering the details of the story.

The captains believed they impressed Native people
with their power and guns and mirrors and coins
and beads, but they didn't even earn a winter count.

Praise Song

York's hunting shirt

York be the strongest, blackest man
anybody this side of the big river has ever seen.
He might show his strength, strut, dance a jig,
or even tease the Indian children,

but he never brag 'bout that what make him
even more proud, that what connect him
to his true man-self, what the natives respect
him most for, his prowess and feats as a hunter.

What other slave you know carry a gun and a hatchet
and a knife sharp enough to split a man's ribs and still
his heart, but be too self mastered to even think on it?
Useful tools, knives and guns, but ain't no magic in them.

The magic was in York. He had the power.
How else you figure a man, twice as big as some,
larger than most, step in among the dead leaves
and wild things and simply disappear?

How else you think he walk right up on wild game
have it sniff the air, tweak its ears
and still not see him less than a touch away?
Standing as still as an oak. Breathing like the forest.

How you reckon he never bring home anything tough
and hard to chew, muscles still in shock from fear
or struggle? He took his game with so much speed
and skill the animals thought they was still alive.

Wrapped around him like a second skin, I hugged him
back into his true self, merged my scent with his,
transformed one of the ancestor's fiercest gifts—reduced
to a white man's slave—back into a real man again.

I swallowed his sweat when he fought with the great
grizzly bear. I felt his heart slow down as he walked
among herds of buffalo. He and I engaged in the dance
of hunting before his blade made the kill.

Like all before me, my two-tone skin is rich and thick
with the color of tree bark and makes him
one with the earth and bush whether the leaves be
on the ground or in the air.

The smell of the outdoors is ground deep into me:
perfume of grasshopper juice, huckleberries, bitter grasses,
animal dung, and the richness of fresh-turned dirt.
I would not be welcome at the fancy dinner table.

There are pouches of dried roots, coyote anklebones,
buffalo teeth, bear claws, and bird quills piercing
every part of me. I could ride his back for a hundred years
and you still could not tell us from the forest.

My purpose is simple. Protect him from harm, guarantee
he never go hungry, and connect him to the hunters, griots,
and sorcerers coursing through his veins. So I do just that
and raise his name in song.

Hunters' Code

Train a sharp eye an ear.
Travel light.

Pray for a worthy adversary.
Always track game downwind.

Don't waste ball an powder if steel blade will do.
Kill only to eat.

Spare the young an them heavy with calves.
Make the wounds quick an clean.

Don't let the animal suffer.
Give thanks for the hunt.

Pour some water for the ancestors.
Apologize for bringing death to the living.

Leave some behind for the forest.
Taste the tender liver, but always eat the heart first.

Signifying

Signifying

York's hatchet

When my onyx captain mean biz-ness,
when he feel threatened
he don't reach for nothin' small 'n pretty
he don't bother fumblin'
with no powderhorn 'n ball neither.

When the choices be life o' death
he know he need a steel tooth killer like me
that know nothin' 'bout no ticklin'
or caressin'. Gentle ain't never been my song.

When a grizzly need to be stopped
dead in his tracks, already fulla hot lead
an madder for it, he gone reach fo' me
t' silence his gapin' mouth 'n angry tone.

He gone ask my steel kiss t' cleave an gash
t' hew 'n chop like lightnin' strikes.

He gone want me t' get loud 'n mean
to unlock that monster's skull
t' run my tongue 'cross his brain, t' burrow
through his ribcage 'til I can taste his heart

t' fill the air with blood 'n guts
'til dere ain't nothin' left
but a bear skin 'n a pile a steaks.

Ya see, killas only respect killas
neva nothin' weak 'n shiny
neva nothin' that hide 'n spit atcha
from behind trees
from fifty paces 'n maybe tear
a lil' hole in ya flesh.

Nah, killin' is what we do
'n the reason he sleep with his fingers
'round my throat.

Settling Debts

The captains would say Sacagawea's gift
was being sister to the Shoshone chief
who give us horses to cross the all-winter
mountains. They write 'bout her rescuing supplies
out the river an trading her own belt for food.

I will always remember her quiet
an how she kept her boy cub alive
with rattlers an grizzlies an hunger 'bout.
She strong as a rock an never complain
'bout the unkind storms or snow or words.

When Capt. Clark offer to take her boy to raise
I catch myself hoping one a the captains write down
my face, scratch out a small York on paper
after a hunt, wild game strung over my shoulders
so somebody knows I earned some rewards too.

Learning Curve
Sacagawea

When I was stolen as a child
and taken far from home and girlhood
I learn to hate
and I cried all the tears I had.

When I become second wife to Charbonneau
I learn to serve.
He older than my own father
and not ride me hard or long
if I lie still and quiet and swallow all my tears.

When I become a mother to my little hunter
his eyes meet mine and melt my stone heart.
This teaches me to love again but my work doubles itself
and soon I have two men to serve.

Concentric

Concentric

Sacagawea

The white man seem to always move and think
in straight lines, while my people put everything
in a circle, including York.

I laugh quietly when I hear the party complain
that when the "savages" circle up it's hard to know
who is in charge. As if even a circle need a captain.

Then I reflect on how a full moon, the bright sun
ball, and even my son's hungry mouth all seem
round and perfect as the way my people see things.

Common Ground

Common Ground

Sacagawea

> As the ocimbamba seeks the low lying tree so friends
> gather to the friendly person.
>   —*African Proverb*

When I follow my husband
who agree to be tongue
for the white man
I meet another who serve like a wife

but he is black as an eagle's claw
big as a tree and a man.
Others call him Big Medicine
and the children run and hide in fear

when he round his eyes and show his teeth
but when he look and smile at me
then hold out a night sky for hands
he make me feel safe and warm.

Goodbye to the Ocean

How to Say Goodbye to the Ocean

Sacagawea

When I meet the Great Water
she who the Raven call Yemaya
I close my eyes and feel her fingers
pull me out toward her circle

away from men, birthing a joy
warmer than any I've ever known.
But when I can no longer smell her salt
in the air and her song gets too soft to hear

my own water breaks again, but this time
instead of a brave little hunter or dancer
I give birth to a great emptiness
I know I'll carry on my back forever.

Cutting Back

York's knife

Thunder might spook a horse,
but lightning is the knife that strikes.
Death is never as simple
as that loud-mouthed hatchet makes it out to be.

He's just extra weight
when there's no killing to be done.
Big dumb clumsy chopping
doesn't require thought or skill.

A blade can cut down a tree or a bear or a man,
but what else can it do?
It can't skin a buffalo
or change its wooly back into rawhide.

It's useless when York needs to scale and clean a fish
or lance a wound.
It might hack off a piece of meat
but can it peel the skin off a piece of fruit?

Size means nothing when the right vein
and the blood that courses through it   need separating.
I can take the hair off a man's throat or slice it open
without raising my voice.

These fools sit around the fires all night
pining for the love of a good woman.
And they believe a good woman
is always quiet and small and pretty.

But they aren't ready for a real one like me,
who is as dangerous and useful in the wild
as fire is in the kitchen.

To Honor and Obey

Agreeing to be Capt. Clark's man servant
be something like being married
only in joining with a wife I have some power
an with the captain I have none.

I say agreeing 'cause I had many a opportunity
to escape an run away, but I choose to stay
an to keep our agreement of sorts
though many could never make good sense a that.

Some think I stayed 'cause a fear a being punished
fear a losing my privileges like hunting with a gun
or fear a being treated like a regular field hand
an I reckon there be some truth in alla that.

But fear ain't the only thing keep people wedded.
Once them gets past the wedding night
they figures out who gets to say
an who gets to do.

An that be a easy thing if you believe one born
to rule over the other, but if you starts out in the world
believing it's so, an then come to know later
that it wrong like I did, it can be a bitter root.

I was so angry for mistaking blindness an foolishness
for what I thought was loyalty
I tried to drown myself in whiskey.
I'm shamed that I called myself a man

but was never man enough to question if it be right
to keep a boot on somebody's neck
just 'cause they be black
or just 'cause they be woman.

I be even more shamed for not seeing
the double booting a them that was both.

Primer II

I can read the heart ova woman in her eyes
as easy as a lie in a man's face.

The direction an power ova storm speaks
clearly to me from low-flying bird wings.

I can dip my fingers into muddy hoof or toe print
an tell how many a what I'm gone have for dinner.

The thickness a tree bark, walnut hulls, an tobacco worms
tell me how ugly winter gone be.

I knows the seasons like a book. I can read moss, sunsets,
the moon, an a mare's foaling time with a touch.

I would trade all this to know how to scratch out
my name as more than a X,

to have my stories leap off paper as easy as they roll
off my tongue,

to listen to my own eyes,
make the words on parchment say

This man here be York.
He can come an go as he please,

work for hisself, own land, learn his books,
live, an   die free

Part II

Ananse Returns

I introduces Ol' York to coyote
an the best Indian tales I can call back up
from the trip out west

His Rose push him to share one
a her favorites 'bout the keys
an how God give the woman power

over the generations an the kitchen
to even out giving man alla strength
he use to knock her 'round.

I smile knowin' how all these stories
almost makes up for the wisdom
folks who can must gets from books

Later, I thinks back on the look
in Rose's eye an how she stare at me
when the lesson in the story unfold.

On the way over to see my wife
I trys to figure out what she really think
I needs to learn.

Merits of Love

Rose and York's Wife Debate the Merits of Love

> Without love . . . little by little we destroy ourselves.
> —*Chief Dan George, Coast Salish*

What I learnt from being married t' Ol' York is dat
love be like a good story dat you can't neva get tired a.

> What I learnt from his son is dat love is quiet
> an dat it don't talk back.

He didn't learn dat foolishness from us. He learnt dat mess
from his white daddy. York want to be like Massa Clark so
bad he need his own slave t' order an' knock around too.

> A man like my York gets knocked 'round out dere
> all day. If he need t' do a little knockin' when he
> come home, so dat he feel like a man, dat's his right.

Chile it's a heap a difference 'tween serving a man 'cause
he own you an serving one 'cause you want him on you.

> Ain't no diff'rence t' me. Dey both can have us
> anytime dey wants. Ain't no law stoppin' 'em
> from killin' us if dey wants neither. We just
> here t' mind dey kids, spin wool, boil dey clothes
> clean, keeps the root cellar an springhouse full,
> an spread our legs. What use we got wit love?

Chile, you make me wanna cry. You so busy waiting on
some joy in the next life,
you done let dese so-called men kill the only thing
dey couldn't take from you.

Whiskey Talks

> . . . the tales that black York told, when he was
> liquored up, were as long as Missouri and tall as the
> Rockies.
> —*Donald Culross Peattie,* Forward the Nation

I killed hundreds a grizzlies
with my bare hands
though I owns my own gun.

made myself invisible
an walked in the forest
unseen.

danced with buffalo
climbed mountains topped
with snow in the summer

seen dogs that live in holes
in the ground and deer with heads
bigger than horses

chiefs gave me they daughters an wives
an stood guard outside
while I done my business.

Me an Capt. Clark sired sons
with Indian gals. Many tribes
traded for my seed.

My captain gone set me free
an give me a piece a land
for all I done on the expedition.

I'm gone buy my family
go back out west
an live like a king.

We not on this earth
to be slaves.

Real Medicine

Real Medicine

> He who does not know a medicine defecates on it.
> —*African Proverb*

I saw a medicine woman surrounded in smoke
turn a buffalo horn 'round

an use it to suck the illness an blood out
a sick body without so much as making a cut.

I watched a medicine man shake his bear claw
sing a healing song an cry for the evil spirit
that lived in a crippled man to leave him in peace.

In the middle a the night there come a great wind
an thundering hoofs that put our fire to sleep.

When the sun returned the man stood up an walked.

Praying Feets

I ordered my boy York to dance. The Indians seem
amazed that a man so large is so light on his feet.
—*William Clark*

Something like leaving happens
when I be ordered to dance.
Not the pack up camp an go kinda leave

but how things might be if my mind
weren't shackled inside my head
like dreaming but not being asleep.

I might take a puff a tobacco, tie on
a piece a red cloth an wave my hatchet
'round my head to get my mind right.

An once I gets good an loose, I starts
to feel lighter an lighter 'til soon
I hardly weighs nothing at all.

I spends as much time in the air
as on my feet an after a while it's like
my soul be dancing to drums that thunder

an I be a small child on the ground watching
my body follow the music, catch it
then leave it to make its own.

My captain think it make him look more powerful
to order a man such as me to dance
but the Indians see my body move by its own spirit

an not by a white man's hand
raise they voices, sing nothing but praises
an join me in the air.

Murmuration

I seen a flock a large birds
change direction at the same time
as if they be a the same mind
or listen to the same drum
like whirling dancers waiting for the break.

I seen more buffalo than trees
run full out 'cross a valley
shoulder to shoulder hoof to hoof
trample everything under foot

somehow spare a newborn deer
frozen in a wet ball   alone
an hidden
among the high weeds.

Like our people, Indians believe
even the animals share a master drummer
but the captains think we the only ones
that know how to dance.

Out There Watching

How I Know Mamma
Out There Watching

> . . . the succession of curious adventures wore the
> impression on my mind of enchantment.
> —*Meriwether Lewis, June 14th, 1805*

One day I separated from the rest a the party to follow
a group a buffalo that seem to call my name
an this angry low cloud swoop down over the river the way
that lion swoop down on the monkey's back in that story

a Ol' York's, only this lion is big an black like me
full a thunder an lightning, an throwing down iceballs
as big as my fist, so I whistles sharp an loud, gets low an
strokes the shells on the hunting shirt she gimme,
an it fly right over.

Before I can reflect on how lucky I be, it come to me that
Charbono's squaw an her lil' warrior, Jean Baptiste
is now right b'neath that lion's claws, so I stampedes back
for the rescue an finds they barely escapes a surprise flood
that washed away Capt. Clark's compass an Charbono's gun.

I think no more about it 'til I hear that before the cloud
swoop in a bear chased Capt. Lewis full out
the length ova cornfield.
Made him jump in the river to get away.

When he climb out the bear turn into a tyger cat
then into three big bull buffalo
that charge him and chase him away.

Only then do I begins to understand her power.

Wordsmith

The half-breed Frenchmans was something else
an pulled they weight as well as any a the mens

but nobody could best Drewyer
when it come to making his hands talk.

Most white men look stiff when trying to speak
with they hands instead a they lips

but he had a way a using his whole body to
communicate 'tween us an the Indians.

He always use his face an eyes to deepen the message
an could call up an change to any emotion needed

to make his words fly over an cause the Indians to nod.
He could make his body say *buffalo* or *deer* or *bear*.

His hands could be a great bald eagle or a hummingbird.
His arms and neck could call up a snake or a river.

Sometimes 'round the fire we ask him to sign us a story
just for the pleasure a seeing him make the words move.

Devil's Tower and
the Big Dipper

for N. Scott Momaday, Rock Tree Boy

Seven sisters an they brother was playing
in what the Indians call the Black Hills out west

the boy pretend to be a grizzly bear
an chase his sisters 'round an 'round

he play so hard he turn into a real bear
an try to eat the sisters who become afraid an run

when they run past a tree stump it hollas out
an tell the sisters to climb on for protection

when bear catch up the stump begin to grow
an grow an grow 'til he can't reach them no more

bear get angry an scrape up stump with claws
stump turn to rock to protect itself

stump keep growing an the seven sisters get so high
them become the seven stars in the ol' drinking gourd.

Power a Touch

When things was first born

sun touch moon
an pass on light

moonlight touch water
an pass on dance

water move upon the land
an give her hips

hips give birth to trees
an them bear fruit

fruit teach man
to pass on seeds

man plant seeds
an woman become moon

moon get full
give birth to son

Red, Light, and Blue

> William Henry Jackson . . . took a picture of a Nez
> Perce half-breed . . . other Nez Perce told him, was
> the son of William Clark.
>
> —*Alvin M. Josephy Jr.*,
> Lewis and Clark Through Indian Eyes

The hero makers say
the captains try an set
a good example
an be too gentlemanly
or too busy
to lie
with Indian women.

But like Ol' York say
babies always tell
on themselves, especially
when they comes out
with red hair,
whiter skin
than they mamma's
an eyes
the color a the sky.

Field Up

> He who learns teaches.
> —*African Proverb*

When Brotha come back from da journey
colored folk come from miles 'round
an sits on da porch all night
just t'hear stories 'bout da indians 'n da ochian

some a da things he say
gets us yung bucks mighty excited 'n stirred up
'n scares off da olda ones
'specially when he talk a tastin' freedom

what it mean t'be a man
'n how out west they worship
our blackness 'n live married to da lan'
like our people do back in Africa

He have us all struttin' like roostas
our backs straight 'n chins up
'n not rushin' t'grin 'n fetch it when called
boys or chil'ren or uncle or less for a long time.

Rose Shows Her Thorns

Rose Shows Her Thorns

York act like his axe got two heads on it
an' dat he da One who make lightnin' strike
but his thunder ain't no more den a han' clap.

I bites my tongue outta respect fo' his daddy
'cause he parta da blame for eggin' on
dat boy's foolishness all dese years

but I lost my taste for 'im after listenin' to 'im
all night on the porch braggin' to da mens 'bout
sleepin' wit' long haired Indian women

an' how much prettier dey is den us, how much
softer dey skin be an' how dey don't talk back.
How dey treated him like a king an' whatnot.

Like 'at wife a his ain't neva washed his dirty feet.

If he was really my son, he'd know better den actin'
so high an' mighty. A big tree fall just the same
as a little one, only harder.

Just 'cause he ain't out in da field. Just 'cause he follow
Massa Clark 'round like a pet dog an eat da scraps
off his plate, he think he better den the rest a us.

He couldn't hardly get his big head in the door when he left.
Now he back here, tellin' all dem lies, an' claimin' to be a hero
for wipin' a white man's ass alla way to the ochian an' back.

Summer a Peace

I dreams so much about the expedition
I wakes up tasting the air for ochian salt
an take on a load a sadness when I open
my eyes an find that I am not a buffalo.

Even awake my mind carry me back
to the Nez Perce an the peaceful life there.
I miss the time spent playing games
while waiting for the mountain snow to melt.

It lift our spirits to try to outshoot their warriors,
pitch the rings at the stick, an run races on foot
though they was the masters a anything on horseback.

I pray the peaceful times I left is theirs forever
an that freedom is all my lil' York an his mamma
ever know, but I fear it is a empty prayer.

A New York

Ev'rytime I sees a beautiful anything with a mustang heart,
catch the moon with her eye wide open or hear the river
slap a wet rock like a man slap his woman's thigh at night

I close my eyes an see her standing there, naked
just after a hard rain, belly fulla promises
an I suddenly remembers what huckleberries taste like

then I know, it one thing to force a man to remember
his life as a slave, but it another to expect him to forget
such gifts as these.

Dream Catcher

The old woman reach in my stomach
an pull out a horse covered with spots.
She keeps pulling an pulling horses 'til
they numbers four.

Then they ride 'round in a big circle
alla way to where the sun rise
when they gets back to us
they all carrying chiefs.

When I make to stare at them I can see
they all be tied to they horses
an alla the riders is dead except one.
An he is cradling a book a light in his arms.

When the people see the book they cut off
they hair an burn all they medicines an skins
Then they stand together in a long long line
wrapped in thin blankets 'til they fall asleep.

When they wake, somebody has stolen alla land.
Alla buffalo are dead. An half-breeds out number
the trees. When I ask the old woman who did this
she points at me an begins to sing a wailing song.

Part III

End a the Song

When Massa Clark trade in his buckskin
for ruffled shirts, silk hose, and buckled shoes
I knows my gun an hatchet an knife be next

being back inside the stomach a the city
put knots in mine after all I seen an done out west

the thunder a buffalo, the roar ova grizzly, the voices
a the ochian an waterfalls is all dead to me here

out in the wild, I could hear my mamma sing
with each morning sun, here in Louavul an St. Louie
I hear nothing but the sound a money being made,
the crack a the whip, an no music.

Say My Name

Say My Name
York's slave wife

Folks round here wanna call me Auntie,
York's ol' wife, or Massa So an So's niggah wench
Like I ain't got a name a my own.

Dem don't know how hard it be t'put aside
a lil' piece a myself dat nobody can't neva touch
but me, a piece big enuf t'wrestle the long hard days
an keep itself warm at night, without a man 'round.

Dem don't know what it like to stand in the dark
night afta night wrapped in dat buffalo robe he sent
look up at the stars an wonda which ones
is lookin down on him an believe if something bad
happen to him out there   dat I   would feel   it too

When he come home, I don't need him to say he love me
I don't need him to bring me gifts, I just wants him
to hold me close, make like he glad to see me
bend down t'my ear   an whisper   my name.

Unwelcome Guest

York's slave wife

I don't think York knowed
I could see hur too.
Da furst time was in da corna a his eye
while he look far off but stare at
da plate right in front a him.

He didn't say nothin' bout hur
but da way his lips turnt up at da ends
said plenny.

I ain't one t'sass. His growl help me
to know a slave woman's place
so I sits up all night wit both my hands
an ears open, waitin' t'catch hur name
on his lips.

Afta dat, no matta how much he talk
a grizzlies, buffalos, big fish,
mountains, or ochians
she become all I can see
all I wants t'know

It gets so crowded in our lil' place
I swears I can almost smell hur.
An by den I knows one a us will have t'go.

Sunflower Seed Oil

The Sunflower Seed Oil Conjure

York's slave wife

First, I gets some fresh well wada
an puts it on t'boil
stirs up a tea brewed from
apricot vine, rattlesnake weed
an plenny a honey.

Den I sets him down 'tween my knees
an wit a wooden tooth comb
left t'me by my mamma's mamma
commences t'scratchin at his scalp
'til his shouldas look covad wit snow.

Den I fills up my wash tub wit
boilin' wada doctored wit peppermint root
an sets to scrubbin' him slow enough
fo' the heat t'open his doors.

When his body is clean I starts back t'work
on his head
bustin up a mean suds and usin'
my fingas to walk up an down his scalp
'til he let loose a low moan
an his eyes start t'roll 'round in his head.

Afta I rinses an twists alla forest out
I starts back in wit warm sunflower seed oil
only dis time ev'ry finga make its own lil' circle
while both m'hands make bigga ones

an they follows each otha from da stiff tree limbs
in da back a his neck, cross his crown
t'his soft spot while my thumbs dig in
slow an deep where da headaches come on.

I pours da extra oil inta my hans an rub
his neck an shouldas, down t'his ribs
an arms den like a turtle dance
I moves back up again.

I works slow an hard an afta a while
when I gets alla way t'his man sack
he open his eyes an be glad its me.

Chapel a Love

Chapel a Love

York's slave wife

> A woman who has a good marriage is said to sleep
> in a good bed.
> —*African Proverb*

After a tin a apricot vine tea
us use the buffalo skin
as the earth
an pile a bunch a quilts

into something like
a handmade sky
an makes us a real
lodge a sweat

If it based on how much
calling on God
come forth
in the dark

what married people do together
on bended knees
once dem work past dey anger
can be holy too.

To Have and to Hold

It do more harm than good
to be enslaved an agree to love forever
when there be folks over us
with even more power than death
to do   us part.

Being another man's property
alls I can promise is
when we in the same quarters
no one will hold you closer
or with more tenderness than me.

If ever I have to choose between
another day a service an death
I will always choose livin'.

Even if Massa sell me down
the Mississippi tomorrow
or pair me up with another woman
to breed

I will only think on what we had
an chase away thoughts
a what we had not.

I aims to see you ev'ry Sunday an Christmas
but if ever I'm away more than two whole
seasons without sending back word,

untie the ribbons from that broom we jump
mourn for me but a little
then set your mind to figuring
on how you gone stay warm
when winter come.

Real Costs
York's slave wife

Somewhere out dere
he learnt t'touch me
like I'm a woman
an not just some woman.
Me.

In our marriage bed
he seem as intrested
in pleasing me as he be
in spillin' hisself.

I knew he come back
changed
when new words
fall out his mouf like
love an freedom
an manhood.

An dere come a look
in his eye
like he own all three
free an clear
an don't need no papers
t'prove it.

But it scare me
'cause I seent dat look

in many a black eye
b'fo white hammas
nailed it shut
o' left it frozen open
an swingin'
t'teach da rest
what anything dat smell
like courage cost.

I have no doubt
he give his life t'stay
wit me
so I don't tell 'im dat Massa
takin' me back
down south.

I just kiss him soft t'sleep
an stare at him long enough
t'call up his face
when I gets old an thankful
he still be breathing
somewhere
when winta come.

Seeing is Believing

Ol' York

Slow by slow we all try on the white man's Jesus
needing something after throwing away Oludumare
an alla gods us come here wit', believing they left us first

but it clear to me dat a faith dat ask a man an his woman
to bow down an serve anotha man an his chil'ren
just 'cause he white, work betta fo' Massa than him slaves.

The old ones say that in Ile-Ife, in the beginning
us danced our faith. We didn't sit like rows a corn
to listen to a white man say how good the next life be.

'Legba, the trickster be ev'rywhere in this place
blocking alla roads, forcing us to call on the Orisas
in ones 'n twos or hide them up under angels 'n saints.

Part IV

Prenupt Agreement

1 president's dream
plus 2 captains
almost 3 dozen men
one 15 year old Indian wife
her baby
a slave

plus
one 55 foot keelboat
2 pirogues
176 pounds of gun powder
420 pounds of sheet lead for bullets
not enough whiskey

minus gifts a 12 dozen pocket mirrors
4,600 sewing needles
10 pounds a sewing thread
130 plugs a tobacco

for 'bout 15 miles per day
for 3 years
an over 8,000 miles

equal 2 heros
double pay for all
320 acres a land for the men
1600 acres for the captains
an
nothin' for York.

His Own Domain

Master of His Own Domain
William Clark

> Give (a slave) a bad master and he aspires to a good
> master; give him a good master, and he wishes to
> become his own master.
> —*Frederick Douglass*

I love my servants as much or more
than my friend Lewis
loved his fine Newfoundland, Seaman.

They have become so much a part of this family
it would grieve me mightily to lose any
or to have to sell them off.

I have had to give the lash to almost all my people
since my return,
as they had developed a most sour attitude
which had begun to affect their work.

Any interruption of work
or challenging of my authority
costs me time and money.

I have never cut off a limb or finger,
starved near to death, cuffed women in irons,
or beat any of my negroes stupid like other men.

I provide for their food, clothing, shelter, and medical care.
I treat them like my own children
until they are buried in the grave.

Others think me cruel for not granting manumission
to my boy, York, but what rational business man
would cut a hole in his own purse?

Five Things

Five Things I Don't Know
William Clark

> I fear you will think I have become a severe master.
> —*William Clark*

I don't know why he thought
he had earned his freedom.

I don't know why he thought
he was more than just a slave.

I don't know why he won't just quit
that woman of his.

I don't know why God made them as easy
to train as mules but twice as ungrateful.

I don't know why he insists
on making me prove who's boss.

Homing Signals

If freedom mean never again
hearing one a Ol' York's stories,
never fussing with his Rose,
or getting to hold my wife an family

If it mean never laughing or hunting
with my brothers Juba an Scippio
or teasing Daphny an Nancy
than it not be something
I would barter for.

None a us be free
lessen alla us gets to come an go
as we please.

I never run 'cause alla my family
still belong to Capt. Clark.

Too Many Wifes and None
Rose

I wish I could feel bad for dat boy, York,
but I can't. He had some hurt comin'.
I feel bad for his wife though,
no tellin' what she gone have t' do
t' survive down south.
Blisterin' sun an' cotton fields
ain't no place fo' a woman.

She was a lil' foolish fo' choosin' him,
but a good wife is what she was, too good
fo' his heavy hands an pigheaded ways.
After she gone, maybe he'll 'preciate
what he had. He did his share a knockin'
an' now he gettin' his on both ends.

Dat fool really only love the forest,
an up 'til he come back here still a slave,
was a pretty good wife to Massa Clark,
but don't tell Ol' York I said dat.
If dat boy fell off a cliff
his daddy say "look at my boy fly,"
an' get mad if you say diffrent.

Brotherly Love

Brotherly Love
Jonathan and Edmund Clark

> I don't like him nor does any other person in this
> country.
> —*Edmund Clark*

The great expedition to the Pacific
secured our brother's career in politics
but made a monster of his boy York.

He and Lewis returned as national heroes
and York was so full of himself you'd have thought
he led the trek.

He strutted around here stirring up Negroes
and looking good, decent pillars of our society
right in the eye.

He threw everything away he'd been taught
and walked and talked as if seeing the ocean
had made him a white man.

Brother trounced him severely
and even had him thrown in the caleboos for his
impudence and drunkenness in St. Louis.

Somewhere out there he forgot his duties as a slave.
He took advantage of our brother's weakness
for him and set a terrible example for the others.

We'd as soon see him sold south to New Orleans
or run north rather than have him around to poison
all our good Negroes.

Many Voices

When I says good-bye to my wife
a voice tell me to squeeze
an hold her tight 'cause I ain't
never gone see or hold her again.

Don't know how I knowed
but since Ol' York took me into the woods
an introduce me to manhood
something like the truth whispers parts
a all my tomorrows an tell me things
I learns to keeps mostly to myself.

Sometime it be my Mamma's voice
an sometime it sound like mine only wiser
warning me a danger
preparing me for a coming death
or reminding me that this body here just be a shell
that Massa might laugh at or work to death
but never know

that inside it be a buffalo
an inside the buffalo be a rock
an inside that rock be a mountain.

Irreconcilable Differences

I does all I can
to help Capt. Clark
get it in his head
that I have had my fill
a our union.

When he raise his hand
to strike me
for the last time
he still have hope
he can make me mind

he believe what we had
is worth saving an that
a new pair a boots
will make it all better.

But he soon know
that he can not whip this man
into a boy again
when he stare me down
an see somebody new
in my eyes.

When he see me dressed
in my hunter's shirt
he make quick plans

to send me back to Kentucke
curse himself for his "weakness"
an vow to never speak my name
again.

Lessons and Ghosts

Lessons and Ghosts

We start as fools and become wise through
experience.
                              —*African Proverb*

I use to think it be the job a the man
to keep his woman in line with a open hand

I use to think there be such a thing
as a good massa and that freedom
be a ghost in a dream that I couldn't touch

I use to think I was too big to be knocked down
too old to learn something new
and too hard on the inside to shed a tear

I use to think that love was a word
that could only be used by white folks

I been wrong on all counts
an I gots plenty scars to prove it.

Queer Behavior

Queer Behavior

Lewis went into a terrible depression. In courting
a wife, his advances were rejected. Jefferson
appointed him Governor of Upper Louisiana, but he
proved utterly unsuited to politics. . . . His decline
eventually ended in suicide.

—Stephen E. Ambrose,
Lewis & Clark: Voyage of Discovery

Why a fancy, educated man, who worked directly
with the president, traveled without harm to the ochian
returned as a hero, made chief a all the new territory
be given to such deep dark sadness, I can't say.

But something give Capt. Lewis cause to question alla
his success, something bigger than all them books
something heavy as a mountain burrowed deep inside
him like a groundhog an emptied out all his joy.

After watching how careful he conduct himself
'round the men an learning how much he frown
on lying with Indian women, I starts to think
'bout the things the men whispered 'round the fire.

I thinks not on if it true, but on how hard it must be
to live life like it not, to walk 'round under a mask
to ignore your own nature, to smile an laugh an dance
for the pleasure a others while crying all on the inside.

Maybe his sorrow was born from fear a his feelings
or maybe he be even more afraid a what others
might think or say. I knows well how a thing like death
seem welcome when you can't hold the ones you love.

Ol' York say, if ain't nothing in the barn but roosters
won't be no eggs for breakfast. But I ain't signifying
I'm just speculating on what ignorance an whiskey say
when they see how he carry hisself an how clean

an orderly he like his things. An it stand to reason
to ask if blue blood an education an manners can explain
all his odd ways or if he just seem a lil' less manly
standing next to a rugged man like Capt. Clark.

All I can rightfully say is he was rich an white an a man
in a land where them three things mean nothing but power.
Why else would he take his own life, unless one a those
things wasn't true, unless he too   was a slave.

Til Death Do Us Part

Til Death Do Us Part

William Clark

> Death will come, always out of season.
> —*Big Elk, Omaha Chief*

When asked in '32 what ever happened to my boy York,
I spoke the truth as far as I know it and even shed a tear.

I ended the gossip and told them he failed in business
and died of the cholera in Tennessee while trying to return
to me and his position as my valued servant.

And why wouldn't he crawl back and apologize
for his foolish behavior over a woman
and for his poor conduct, instead of returning west to live
among the savages?

I was prepared to welcome him with open arms.
I would have history know
that I was not nor am I a severe master.

I understood the inferior nature of the slave.
His emotional and intellectual development
being what it was,

York couldn't forget all the nonsense put in his head
about his blackness
nor appreciate freedom
or understand the true place and value of women.

It was my idea to take him along to serve
on the great expedition.
It ruined a good slave. It ruined a great relationship.
And that kills me.

Weighing a the Heart

There be a voice inside that speak
only when I feels guilty
for something ugly

that come on my heart or 'cross my mind
an even louder when I acts on it
an say or do a thing I later regrets.

I remembers that Ol' York say
a piece a God live in every good man
an be what some calls a soul

then I look at alla wrong
I done an wonder how bad it scar
my soul to know a devil in there too.

But how easy some men must sleep
them having no guilt
an little soul.

Umatilla Prophecy

Our people will be herded like buffalo
and walked backward from their own lands
until they fall off a great cliff.

Coyote will pretend to fall with them
and offer firewater and guns and beads
in exchange for their tongues and wisdom.

Young warriors will trade their best ponies
for white man clothes and iron horses.
Many will forget the hunt and the sweat.

Our storytellers will stop the winter count.
The rivers will turn to stone.
The white man will write down our truths.

But when they gather in great numbers
to celebrate their long trip to the ocean and back
many tribes will open their eyes and speak as one.

Before our feet touch the ground
we will grow eagle wings and buffalo horns
fly back to our homelands and rescue our stories.

The mountains will see us coming and weep.
The rivers will see us coming and sing.
The salmon will see us coming and dance with joy.

Gye Nyame

Gye Nyame

Ol' York say Africans believe a person can only die
when the people no longer speak they name.

I give you these words to hold, not so you remembers mine
but so you know the truth an keeps it alive as well.

He say there be times in every man's life when he have to
choose to hunt to feed himself or to hunt to feed his people

but only once can he choose to hunt no more forever.
He say when it all said an done there be nothing left 'cept
God.

Vision Quest III

In my dream I am standing in a deep deep hole
surrounded by a herd a wooly-headed buffalo

an hands as big as mine
are throwing dirt on my body.

At the edge a the hole
a old white man wrapped in a flag

is standing with his back turned away
an writing in a book with a long gold quill.

High above me in the clouds
an eagle is flying in circles.

When she folds her wings and starts to dive
I feel my body begin to float toward the surface

Her screeches are loud and piercing
They vibrate everything above and below the water.

She screeches one final time just before she plucks me
out of the river and carries me away, dancing like a fish.

Like Heroes

is how the party was treated
when we returned
even me, back in the quarters

truth is
we ran out a food an supplies
before we even reached the ochian
we stole horses an anything else we could use

we pried the legs a women an girls open
let them think we had something special
something powerful to leave
with the trail a half-breeds
an sores an sickness

drunk with power an arrogance
we killed some young Blackfeet boys
then hung a peace medal 'round they neck

truth is
Indians was better people than us

instead a killing us all
they give us comfort an food
when we was starving

guides an directions
when we was lost

they traded their horses an women
for our survival an pleasure

watched us stumble all the way
to the ochian an back

we got better than we deserved from them

they got a whole lot worse

Time Line

1770	William Clark is born
ca. 1772	York is born
1799	John Clark (William Clark's father) dies. William Clark inherits York and other slaves
1801	Meriwether Lewis becomes personal secretary to newly elected president Thomas Jefferson
1803	United States acquires Louisiana from France
Summer 1803	Clark accepts Lewis's invitation to be coleader of expedition
October 14, 1803	Lewis arrives in Louisville
October 26, 1803	Lewis, Clark, York, and the nine young men from Kentucky leave the Falls of the Ohio
May 14, 1804	The Corps leaves the winter camp at Wood River
August 20, 1804	Sgt. Charles Floyd dies
February 11, 1805	Sacagawea's son, Jean Baptiste Charbonneau (Pomp), is born
November, 1805	Lewis and Clark–led parties reach the Pacific Ocean
March 23, 1806	The return trip begins
May 3, 1806	The party returns to Nez Perce

	village for horses; forced to fall back until snow thaws in the Bitterroots
July 3, 1806	Led by Nez Perce guides, the party breaches the mountains
August 17, 1806	Party leaves Sacagawea, Pomp, and Charbonneau at Mandan village
September 23, 1806	The party arrives in St. Louis to a cheering crowd
Nov. 5, 1806	Lewis, Clark, and York arrive back in Louisville
Oct. 11, 1809	Lewis dies in Tennessee from an apparent suicide
1811–1816	York works as a wagoner in Louisville
Dec. 20, 1812	Sacagawea dies
1815	York works for drayage business formed by William Clark and his nephew, John Hite Clark
1832	In interview with Washington Irving, Clark reports York's death
1838	Clark dies in St. Louis

Another Trek
York's Nez Perce Legacy

After an evening reading at Summer Fishtrap, a writing conference held every year in Nez Perce country at the foot of the Wallowa Mountains, just outside Joseph, Oregon, I stepped outside of a wooden cabin nestled near the opposite end of beautiful Wallowa Lake and the grave site of legendary Nez Perce leader Chief Joseph. There I met Diana Mallickan, a park ranger stationed in Spalding, Idaho, on the Lapwai reservation, and Allen Pinkham, an important Nez Perce elder and former chair of the tribe's governing body. I was holding my breath in anticipation of a critique of my book of poems entitled *Buffalo Dance: The Journey of York* (Lexington: University Press of Kentucky, 2004).

I had already survived criticism from Lewis and Clark enthusiasts and history scholars, but the audience I feared the most, representative voices of people most absent in the telling of the Lewis and Clark saga, now stood before me in the dark. I braced myself for the worst but breathed a sigh of relief when Pinkham held out a hardback copy of *Buffalo Dance* for me to sign.

The private and warm exchange that began that night continued over several years and grew to include a public reading at the University of Idaho, in Moscow, and an invitation to visit and read from the York manuscript at Lapwai High School, a Native American secondary school on the reservation. The initial meeting at Fishtrap also led to an opportunity to present my poems during the signature event of the National Lewis & Clark Bicentennial Commemoration at Lewis and Clark College and again in St. Louis for the commemoration's final event, called Currents of Change.

After a series of visits back to the reservation in Lapwai, including numerous visits with my son, D'Van, in tow, we were invited to play basketball, attend a powwow and a sweat lodge, and to dine with members of the Nez Perce tribe.

On one of our northwest excursions, having already followed the Lewis and Clark Trail along the Columbia River all the way to the Pacific, my son and I drove north from the reservation to Coeur d'Alene, Idaho, and over to Travelers Rest, Montana, then followed the Bitterroot River back through the mountains to the reservation. We traveled over rugged Lolo Pass, following the old buffalo trail that served as part of the official Lewis and Clark trail and features hot springs and unspoiled views that York himself must have seen. Every incredible vista, meal, and personal encounter with the Nez Perce proved invaluable, but the greatest gift of all was the invitation to visit the Nez Perce National Historical Park Research Center's library and archives at the Spalding station. I knew I was in sacred space when an archivist pulled up several computer images of Harlem Renaissance–era Native American jazz bands in war bonnets and full native regalia. Most important for my work was the discovery that the archives housed, among other treasures, transcribed oral history related to York's time spent with the Nez Perce.

The materials in the archives relating to York not only echoed the same welcome spirit that my son and I experienced during our visits, they also revealed information previously unrecorded in all my earlier research on York and the Lewis and Clark expedition. Important facts, not present in the Lewis and Clark journals, indicate that York, Clark, and other members of the party took native "wives" and, in many cases, fathered children during the time spent with various tribes. These records finally addressed, head-on, rumors that historians have heretofore carefully avoided and ceremoniously dismissed in almost every historical treatment of the expedition. The archival material specifically detailed a recognized public relationship between York and the daughter of Chief Red Grizzly that resulted in the birth of a son, also named York. The transcribed history described their courtship, including canoe rides on the Clearwater River.

Moreover, during our visits to the reservation, we had several meals with known descendents of York, a feat ironically impossible in Kentucky and Virginia, where such descendents are not publicly recognized. The legacy of devaluing the families and marriages of enslaved individuals like York continues today; his slave wife's name, for example, is still absent from our history books, along with all references to any children they might have borne together.

It was also at Fishtrap where I met the late Marc Jaffe, who was working with Alvin M. Josephy Jr. on an important anthology of Native voices called *Lewis and Clark Through Indian Eyes* (New York: Knopf, 2006), which included essays by Allen V. Pinkham Sr., N. Scott Momaday, Roberta Conner, and other recognized Native American writers, scholars, and leaders. This collection would prove extremely useful in helping to shift the focus in the public discourse around the importance of the great trek to include a Native perspective, just as the bicentennial commemoration was coming to a close.

The information contained in the transcribed oral histories from the Nez Perce I had encountered, in addition to *Lewis and Clark Through Indian Eyes,* forced me to take another look at the voices from this story that were, after all this time, still silent. These resources encouraged me to begin looking at the Lewis and Clark expedition again, but this time through the lens of the women in York's life—specifically his Nez Perce wife and his slave wife, whose voices provide the emotional undercurrent in this latest retelling of the journey.

I tried to look for light wherever the poetic prism led. Many works helped me to re-enter the space these poems come from. There were general sources on the expedition, such as The National Council of the Lewis & Clark Bicentennial's brochure called *A Guide to Visiting The Lands of Many Nations & to the Lewis & Clark Bicentennial*; NebraskaLand Magazine's *America Looks West: Lewis and Clark on the Missouri,* 80, no. 7 (2002);

and the more specialized *Or Perish in the Attempt: Wilderness Medicine in the Lewis & Clark Expedition*, written by David J. Peck (Helena, Mont.: Farcountry Press, 2002).

The scholarly work of Dr. Jim Holmberg's *Dear Brother: Letters of William Clark to Jonathan Clark* proved invaluable, and Ken Burns's film on the expedition entitled *Lewis & Clark: The Journey of the Corps of Discovery* (PBS, 1997) continued to help me to visualize the landscape all the way from Kentucky to the Pacific when I needed to re-see what I was writing about.

To reacquaint myself with the voices of the participants, I looked again at *The Journals of Lewis and Clark*, edited and abridged by Anthony Brandt (Washington, D.C.: National Geographic Adventures Classics, 2002); as well as the journals of expedition member Patrick Gass, *The Journals of Patrick Gass, Member of the Lewis & Clark Expedition*, ed. Carol Lynn MacGregor (Missoula, Mont.: Mountain Press Publishing Company, 1997), which provided an additional point of view. Robert B. Betts's *In Search of York* (Boulder: The University Press of Colorado, 2000) was important in exploring the main character of my story.

Books on slavery, such as Dorothy and Carl J. Schneider's *An Eyewitness History of Slavery in America From Colonial Times to the Civil War* (New York: Facts on File, 2000); Velma Mae Thomas's *Lest We Forget: The Passage from Africa to Slavery and Emancipation* (New York: Crown Publishers, 1997); and the primary sources contained in John W. Blasengame's *Slave Testimony: Two Centuries of Letters, Speeches, Interviews, and Autobiographies* (Baton Rouge: Louisiana State University Press, 1977) were crucial to the voices I wanted to develop. Additionally, Joseph M. Murphy's *Santeria: African Spirits in America* (Boston: Beacon Press, 1993) helped me to address this necessary component of the narrative.

There were many sources that helped to contextualize the Native American voices and lives I wished to know better, including Edward S. Curtis's *Native American Wisdom: Photographs by Edward S. Curtis* (Philadelphia: Running Press, 1994); William

S. Lyon's *Encyclopedia of Native American Healing* (New York: W. W. Norton & Co., 1996); Peter Nabokov's edited volume, *Native American Testimony: A Chronicle of Indian-White Relations From Prophecy to the Present, 1492–2000*, rev. ed. (New York: Penguin Books, 1999); and Kent Nerburn's edited collection, *The Wisdom of the Native Americans* (Novato, Calif.: New World Library, 1999). In considering the Native American experience of the expedition, however, no resource was more significant than the original oral histories of the Nez Perce themselves, transcribed by Baird, Diana Mallickan, and Swagerty, "Voices in Nez Perce," vol. II.

Wading through these many volumes, traveling the thousand-plus miles to the ocean and back, sitting in the sweat lodge, walking the same riverbanks and staring up into the same big sky that embraced York, and spending time with the same beautiful people that made a home for him is the reason these poems breathe air. I pray my own feeling and beliefs don't get in the way of the voices of the individual voices assembled here, which must speak their own truths.

Acknowledgments

Special thanks to my research assistant/partner/wife, Michaele L. Pride. Thanks for the feedback and eyeballs of Mitchell Douglas, Jim Minick, Parneshia Jones, Drew Dillhunt, James Holmberg, CX Dillhunt, Tim Seibles, Greg Pape, Debra Magpie Earling, and Vivien Ara. Thanks to Cheryl Floyd-Miller for the brilliant, probing questions. Thanks to Diane Malikan, Allen Pinkham, Jeff Guillory, and the Nimiipuu (Nez Perce Nation) for welcoming me to the Rez, Lapwai High School, and the sweat lodge. Thanks to Roberta Conner, Pam Steele, Brian Conner, the Lewis and Clark Trail Heritage Foundation, the Lewis and Clark Interpretive Center in Great Falls, Montana, and the Tamástslikt Cultural Institute. Thanks to Laurel Lightner for light. Thanks to the Cave Canem family for continuing to raise the bar and to the Affrilachian Poets for holding up their end. Thanks, Faith, for your continued presence and blessings, and the Lannan family in Santa Fe, and Marfa for the generous support and encouragement to find these poems, and the wonderful staff at the University Press of Kentucky and Deborah Meade for carving this collection into a book. Aché.

About the Author

Frank X Walker is the author of three collections of poetry: *Affrilachia; Buffalo Dance: The Journey of York;* and *Black Box*. He is the founding editor and publisher of *PLUCK! The Journal of Affrilachian Arts & Culture*. A founding member of the Affrilachian Poets and a Cave Canem Fellow, he received the prestigious 2005 Lannan Foundation Poetry Fellowship. His other awards and honors include honorary doctoral degrees from Transylvania University and University of Kentucky, the 2004 Lillian Smith Book Award for *Buffalo Dance*, a Kentucky Arts Council Al Smith Fellowship, and the 2006 Thomas D. Clark Award for Literary Excellence. A graduate of the University of Kentucky and Spalding University's MFA in Writing Program, he is Lecturer of English and Writer in Residence at Northern Kentucky University.